HAIR
OF THE
DOG

HAIR OF THE DOG

80 HANGOVER COCKTAILS AND CURES

SALVATORE CALABRESE

STERLING EPICURE
New York

*To my good friend and bookmaker, the late Lynn Bryan,
with whom I had the pleasure of working with on this
and so many other books.*

STERLING EPICURE
New York

An Imprint of Sterling Publishing Co., Inc.
1166 Avenue of the Americas
New York, NY 10036

Originally published in the UK in 2003

ISBN 978-1-4549-3428-8

Distributed in Canada by Sterling Publishing Co., Inc.
c⁄o Canadian Manda Group, 664 Annette Street
Toronto, Ontario M6S 2C8, Canada
Distributed in the United Kingdom by GMC Distribution Services
Castle Place, 166 High Street, Lewes, East Sussex BN7 1XU, England
Distributed in Australia by NewSouth Books
University of New South Wales, Sydney, NSW 2052, Australia

For information about custom editions, special sales, and premium
and corporate purchases, please contact Sterling Special Sales at
800-805-5489 or specialsales@sterlingpublishing.com.

Manufactured in Canada

2 4 6 8 10 9 7 5 3 1

sterlingpublishing.com

Cover design by Igor Satanovsky
Interior design by Gavin Motnyk

Image credits: Getty Images/iStock: ranplett (background): cover; Zdenek Sasek (stick man):
cover, throughout; **Shutterstock**: josep perianes jorba (beverage icons): cover, throughout

CONTENTS

PREFACE

I t's 2 a.m. and you are having the time of your life. "The night is young!" you hear yourself cry; the club is heaving with people and the vibes are definitely as good as that bottle of Cabernet you drank at dinner. On your arm is a sweet young thing, skin soft and sensual. "More wine, my good waiter!" you say clearly, although he doesn't quite understand your drunken enunciation and delivers two bouncers and a taxi instead.

The next day, daylight breaks through a chink in the blind. You wince as your eyelids begin to flutter. You try to lift your head and something inside recalls the wine, the music, and the sparkling wine . . . and your head pleads with you to lie back on the pillow. Trying to lift your arm proves difficult. It's heavy—too heavy. So are your legs; someone has super-glued you to the sheets. Your brain's flickering like a dance-floor light show and your thoughts keep flashing instructions: *sleep, sleep, sleep . . .*

This familiar scenario is played out every day throughout

the world by millions of men, women, and teenagers, and has been doing so ever since we started counting off the centuries. It first happened to me when I was seventeen. After an evening of titanic drinking, waking up the next day was a nightmare. My mother took one look at me and knew I was in need of her magical potion. My head was spinning, my stomach churning—I thought I was going to die. Actually, I *wanted* to die. It was the easiest, painless way out.

The first thing I recall was the smell of freshly made coffee, and my mother's voice calling me: "Salvatore . . ." I didn't want to wake up; I just wanted to sink deeper into my sorrowful state. However, my mother has a remedy for everything. I slowly opened one eye and looked in the direction of the smell of the coffee. A small espresso was waiting for me. I knew the coffee wouldn't help everything, but it would stimulate me to wake up. I stumbled into the kitchen, where my mother was busy creating her tried-and-tested rescue remedy. I still remember it today and recommend it to anyone. (See Rosa's Magical Cure on page 76.) One glass and I knew I would live to face another day.

Since the age of eleven, I have worked in the bar business. Bartenders are many things to many people: friend, psychiatrist, good listener, entertainer, but above all, he or she is also a doctor—a wizard who uses the bar as a pharmacy to create magical potions to save the world.

Alcohol affects people in different ways. It delivers various symptoms ranging from a headache to excruciating nausea and a general weakness. A hungover person's eyes are droopy; they're tired and listless. Even if they're impeccably dressed, they still look ragged around the edges. They can't sit up straight, but their body language reflects the internal damage done the night before. It's then they always want the impossible: an instant cure.

This is more complicated than it sounds. When you're talking cure, you have to consider what you drank and how much. What are the symptoms: Is it the splitting headache, or does your stomach wish it were elsewhere? Or are you just generally unwell?

To a bartender, many of the bottles on the shelf behind the bar are a source of comfort. Remember, some of the many alcoholic beverages sold today were originally made as preventatives and cures for all kinds of illnesses. These potions include Chartreuse, Fernet Branca, gin, brandy, Angostura bitters—even Campari if you mix it with the right ingredient. Jazz maestro George Melly has been known to imbibe a Campari and soda each morning after the gig the night before. "It gives a slight sense of taking medicine and cleans the throat," he says. "The bitter taste has the virtue of making one feel virtuous while restoring a certain sense of well-being."

There are so many tales I could tell you of completely wasted people limping into my bar. Here's just one of the more positive stories: A regular customer once held a bachelor party at the hotel where I worked. His friends took him over the edge. When he came to the bar the next morning, dressed for the ceremony, he was sweating, shaking, and looked in a terrible state. He needed instant help. I asked for the symptoms; luckily, it was mainly his stomach and a lack of energy. A Calabrese Blood Transfusion was the only solution (see page 48).

"This will either cure you or kill you before your fiancée gets the chance. Whatever, you'll make it to the altar," I said as I passed it to him. He survived. And surviving is the name of the game when you encounter a hangover. I tell customers that it's wise to remember they had a great time getting into this state. Memory is a very important psychological tool, and good memories will help you through any fog.

Chemistry is also useful. One day a doctor came into the bar and gave me a recipe to follow: a Mexican concoction, which I later discovered was the recipe for a Vampiro (page 81). I thought it peculiar, chopping raw onion with chili and mixing tomato with orange juice, but I followed it to the last milliliter. When he'd drunk two of these, I saw a person re-born before my eyes. He perked up, thanked me, and left. *Voila!* I had learned that spices, onion, and garlic, with the addition of vitamins from the juices, help build natural defenses, aided by a little hair of the dog.

I spent the next few years experimenting with various recipes for cures, the investigation of which, to me, is one of the most interesting aspects of my job. I have tried recipes from all over the world: Russia, the Far East, Australia, the U.S. All are interesting but none of them provide a cure. In Italy, we drink and eat. Eating helps the body during a drinking session—it absorbs the alcohol. It doesn't prevent you from getting drunk, but it might give you less of hangover if you drink a lot. We Italians use fresh orange juice and raw eggs as a cure, unlike the Scandinavians, who drink a shot of schnapps with pickled herring. Just the thought makes me feel queasy, but they swear by it.

One last bit of advice. Here are my golden rules for when you have a desperate hangover. The first is, don't talk to anyone. Conversation of any kind guarantees the filing of divorce papers, being fired from your job, and even worse, a loss of face.

Secondly, never read any of those awful Christmas and New Year features on how to avoid hangovers because they're written by puritans who've never had a real humdinger themselves.

Third? Stay sober . . .

HOW A HANGOVER WORKS

uman beings have been in search of a hangover cure ever since wine drinking began in Persia around 5,000 BCE. That first drop of alcohol (taken from a primitive spoon, perhaps) touched a lip, was sipped, savored, and swallowed. That spoon became a drinking vessel as the taste for it developed, then a bottle, and finally, a glass.

By the seventeenth century, rough French wine was being distilled into Cognac, port flowed into England via Portugal, the consumption of gin was ruining more than mothers, and ale and rum were slopping out of tankards (like a stein) throughout Britain and her myriad colonies.

Once the taste of alcohol had become appealing to humankind, the palate took a shine to its various incarnations. Initially, the only alcoholic drink anyone imbibed was limited to whatever foul brew that was developed by crude fermentation. As time marched on, this process became more sophisticated; the cactus gave up its nectar to produce Tequila, grains were transformed into beer, and the Greeks turned grapes into wine (which the Romans later perfected).

Alcohol became a habit, an integral part of a day in the life of anyone with access to a still or the contents thereof. And, as author and drinker F. Scott Fitzgerald noted in his book, *My Lost City:* "The hangover became a part of the day as well allowed for as the Spanish siesta."

WHAT IS A HANGOVER?

While writing this book, I spent many hours wondering who first woke with a splitting headache, an upset stomach, and a mouth like the bottom of a dead parrot's cage to utter those immortal words: "God, I've got a hangover." We shall never know, but at least we can trace the history of the term itself.

The word "hangover" came into common usage at the turn of the twentieth century in the United States. Of course, other countries have their own versions. In Spain, you'd need to whisper *resaca* (originally "malady") to get help; in Italy, *malassere dopo una sbornia* ("malady after a night of too much alcohol"). In Sweden, it's *baksmalla* (after-effect); in Germany, they talk of having a *Katzenjammer* (literally, "the wailing of cats"); in France, it's *gueule de bois* ("wooden throat"), while in the Netherlands, their word of choice is *kater* ("cat").

Whatever the language, "hangover" has become the accepted term for any illness that is caused by too much drink. Physical symptoms include headache, nausea, thirst, fatigue, and sickness,  plus an increased sensitivity to light and sound, bloodshot eyes, muscle aches, vomiting, and sleep disturbance. Blood pressure can be raised, and a rapid heartbeat, tremor, and sweating might also develop. Mental signs include dizziness, a sense of the room spinning, and mood disturbances, especially depression, anxiety, and irritability. These symptoms are universal, and they appear in both male and female sexes. Luckily, not all are present every time you overindulge, and their intensity usually manifests itself in proportion to the amount and type of drink consumed.

Throughout the centuries, many types of quack medicines have been hailed as hangover "cures." At the start of the twenty-first century, there is no definitive cure—but that doesn't mean there aren't people claiming to have invented one. Finding a cure has become an obsession with some pharmaceutical companies. Whoever does invent a foolproof formula, whether it is a combination of natural or chemical ingredients, will have discovered the drinker's Holy Grail. And they will never have to work again.

A hangover cure would change our society beyond all recognition. Absenteeism would drop dramatically. There would be no excuse not to turn up for work. Productivity levels would rise noticeably. Since ninety-two percent of men and eighty-six percent of women drink alcohol—how many hangovers is that a week? No one can put a figure on it, but it doesn't take much imagination to know it's quite a few.

If there were a cure, the problem of the hungover worker would disappear. You know the sort of thing: the office desks remain exactly the same throughout the day as when the workers arrived. All they've done is sleep in the storeroom, having put an almost illegible notice on the door declaring, "No Admittance: Stock-taking in Progress." We all know what they're taking stock of—the levels of toxicity in their blood!

On a more serious note, readers ought to bear in mind that alcohol is the most potent legal narcotic available. You need no prescription for it. Thus, there are some drinkers who have passed from social drinking into the physical disease of alcoholism. Such people, sadly, cannot be helped by this book.

WHAT IS THE EFFECT OF ALCOHOL?

In order to understand the science behind a hangover remedy, it is vital to comprehend exactly what alcohol does to the body. It is also important to understand that each of us reacts differently to alcohol, and we may even have inborn allergic reactions to alcohol.

The type of alcohol we drink is known as ethanol or ethyl alcohol. Initially, it acts as a mild anesthetic. When the first few sips of alcohol arrive in the stomach, gastric enzymes known as alcohol dehydrogenases (ADH) begin to break down the alcohol molecules even before they can be absorbed into the bloodstream. Men generally have a more active pre-absorption mechanism than women, but drinking quickly can bypass the mechanism altogether. Consequently, alcohol slips into the bloodstream and gets whisked away to the brain, where it delivers an initial sense of euphoria as it attacks the membranes of nerve cells known as neurons.

The body can absorb about one ounce of forty percent alcohol by volume (ABV) or eighty-proof spirit an hour. If your body takes in more than one ounce an hour, the brain's motor facilities are upset (via the attack on the neurons), speech becomes slurred, and the muscle control is loosened. The more alcohol you drink, the worse it becomes. You can even fall into a drunken stupor and, if you drink far, far too much, a coma.

When alcohol gets into the bloodstream and enters the liver, the body's "poison filter," it is "metabolized"—meaning that more ADH transforms it into harmless acetic acid via a series of molecular transformations.

First, ADH converts the ethanol molecules into acetaldehyde. Then a second enzyme, known as aldehyde dehydrogenase (ALDH), converts acetaldehyde to acetate. Acetate is harmless, whereas acetaldehyde, a relative of formaldehyde, is extremely toxic.

If all this happens according to plan, about ninety percent of the alcohol you drink will have been metabolized, and the remaining ten percent will pass out of your body via urine and exhaled air. The result? You won't experience any unpleasant effects. Drink more than your body can metabolize, however, and aldehydes, in the form of acetylaldehyde, build up in the body. This overload causes the flushing, nausea, headache, and general feeling of illness that goes hand in hand with drinking too much.

HOW TO READ THE SIGNS

Having waded through some chemistry, how will you know you have a hangover? This (unlike chemistry) is fairly simple. The first symptom is the headache, which is caused by dehydration. Alcohol is a diuretic, sucking moisture from the body's cells, encouraging you to urinate, and thus making your kidneys work overtime. Therefore, you must drink copious amounts of water to replenish your lost stocks. Alcohol also lowers the levels of minerals and vitamins in the body. Calcium and magnesium go off and hide somewhere else, depleting blood

levels, as do the essential salts potassium and sodium. Alcohol also affects levels of vitamins B1, B6, and C.

The second symptom is nausea, caused by too much acid building up in your stomach and irritating its lining. You have ingested a substance (alcohol) that's disruptive to your body. Some of it is poisonous, and your body decides to cleanse itself, often unpleasantly, by making you throw up.

The third symptom is fatigue, caused by the loss of sugar in the form of glycogen, which is stored in the liver. When you drink, the glycogen turns into glucose and departs when you urinate. Your body has to work harder to do what it does normally.

And you were out late, and didn't sleep well. Part of normal sleep is a dream-filled stage, known scientifically as rapid-eye movement, or REM sleep. This is the most important part of a sleep pattern and happens four to five times a night. For obscure reasons, alcohol inhibits REM sleep. As a consequence, you go to bed drunk yet you wake up early, can't get back to sleep, and will be irritable and tired and not worth speaking to the next day.

HOW MUCH IS TOO MUCH?

The one question I am always asked is: How much wine and how many glasses of spirit can one drink without getting hungover? The answer is: How long is a piece of string? Put simply, it depends upon your physiology and your reaction to individual alcohols. We are all individuals and will react differently to different types of alcohol. I know one man who can drink Champagne all day and show no ill effects; another can drink whiskey by the bottle and still be upstanding. However, if I drink a whiskey or two, I know I will feel some ill effects because it is made of grain and I suffer from hay fever. At certain times of the menstrual cycle, alcohol has a greater effect on women than at others. They can drink one glass and have it "go right to their heads."

There are a multitude of other factors to consider. For example, the stronger the wine, the more likely it will be to give you a hangover. The alcoholic content of wine ranges from around nine percent ABV to seventeen percent ABV for a fortified wine. The ABV differs from country to country, and region to region. If wine grapes have been grown on a dry hillside in a warm climate, less water has gone naturally into the grapes—therefore there will be less water in the final wine. I love a robust, deep, rich, red wine, but I know it will have a greater ABV percentage—and consequently a greater effect on my body.

Generally speaking, beer is about 99.9 percent water and has less alcohol by volume than wine or spirits. You can drink more beer than you can vodka and not fall over.

Spirits are usually forty percent ABV, which means they are much stronger than wine when taken neat. Liqueurs are between eighteen and thirty-three percent ABV, except absinthe, which ranges from sixty-eight to seventy-seven percent of pure spirit, and can be quite lethal.

The reason spirits have a more powerful effect is because they stay longer in the bloodstream. The best advice is to read the label of whatever you are about to drink because it will give you the percentage of alcohol and allow you to check your intake.

OTHER TOXIC INGREDIENTS

Just to confuse your body further, the alcohol we take into our systems isn't pure. Many of these impurities, which are known as congeners, are toxic chemicals, either natural or synthetic, that are absorbed during the fermentation or distillation processes, and some spirits and wines have more of them than others. That little glass of sherry sipped before dinner or the teeny glass of port sipped after dinner are congener-rich.

Researchers into the effects of alcohol on the human body have found that the darker the drink, the worse the hangover; similarly, the more transparent your drinks, the fewer problems you will encounter next morning.

Other research has developed a list showing brandy, red wine, rum, and whiskey as the agents that cause the most painful mornings after the nights before. Thus, other facts to consider when "choosing your poison" include the following:

- Vodka has fewer congeners than gin.
- White rum, such as Bacardi, has fewer congeners than dark rum.
- Brandy, rum, and single-malt Scotch have about six times more congeners than gin.
- Bourbon-drinkers ingest eight times the amount of congeners as do gin-drinkers.
- Red wines contain more congeners than white wines.
- Fine wines usually have fewer toxins than cheap wines.

HOW HUNGOVER ARE YOU?

PLEASE, CAN I DIE NOW? ☠ ☠ ☠ ☠ ☠

How it happens: Three gin martinis to start off. Red wine to excess. A large glass of Cognac, followed by a final martini. No food all night. OR: a Champagne cocktail that becomes a "bottle of Champagne." Then a bowl of thin soup; no bread. Then six glasses of red wine, followed by a glass or three of port. Finish the night with three glasses of malt whiskey.

Solution: My heart bleeds for you, but rest assured the room will stop spinning. Eventually . . .

UNBEARABLE ☠ ☠ ☠ ☠

How it happens: A Cosmopolitan to start the evening. Six glasses of white wine. Brandy and more brandy with no food.

OR: About eight glasses of some sort of cheap liquor. (Expensive brands undergo more extensive distillation, which lessens the number of congeners contained.) No food other than chips nibbled early on in the evening.

Solution: Try to remember that there is, in fact, an afterlife.

SUFFERING ☠ ☠ ☠

How it happens: Two whiskey sours followed by several glasses of carbonated (or bubbly) drinks such as sparkling wine, or tonic and soda water in mixed drinks. One final whiskey sour as a nightcap. No food.

Solution: Make sure your drinking partner is ahead of you.

I'LL LIVE ☠ ☠

How it happens: Three sweet drinks (Bailey's and cream, piña coladas, and so on). Sweet flavors disguise the taste of alcohol, and you may not realize how much alcohol you are really consuming.

Solution: Eat a little early in the evening, but check that all your clothes are still in place.

HANGOVER? WHAT HANGOVER? ☠

How it happens: Three vodka and tonics consumed with blinis and smoked salmon. Finally, a large glass of water. No problems!

Solution: Carry on. But watch out for the banana skins . . .

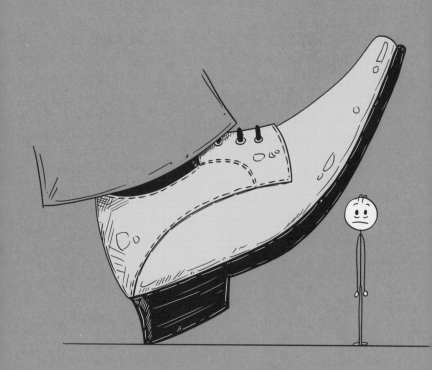

HOW TO PREVENT A HANGOVER

Drink too much and the hangover will always get you. Yet taking the right steps to prevent the worst-possible scenario will help you through the next day.

BEFORE DRINKING

Try to eat a large dinner (or lunch or breakfast, for those of you who start drinking early) because any food will insulate the stomach, slowing the process of alcohol absorption into the bloodstream by letting the digestive enzymes get straight to work. It's best to stick to plain food. As Kingsley Amis writes in his delightful book, *Every Day Drinking*, "Avoid shellfish, greasy meat like pork, anything cooked in butter. Again, no surprises, so save that exciting new Ugandan restaurant for a quiet evening."

Fats and carbohydrates are the best foods for slowing absorption, and sugar intake helps prevent hangovers. Cakes and pastries are the party foods that have lots of all three.

If, like the Italians and the French, you eat starchy foods such as bread, rice, and pasta before and during a drinking session, you will slow the absorption of alcohol into your bloodstream. Your body will be better able to cope with the amount of alcohol you imbibe and it will be able to break it down at a reasonable pace.

DON'T FORGET YOUR COAT

Milk coats the stomach, protecting the lining from any alcohol damage. If you're planning to drink, have a glass before you go do.

In a similar vein, the Lebanese learned the following trick from the Romans. To preserve wine, they floated olive oil on top of it inside its storage vessel. Air didn't penetrate the wine, and thus it was preserved from oxidation, or reacting badly with air. From this observation, they decided that if they drank a teaspoon of olive oil, it would float on top of the stomach and, therefore, protect it from alcohol damage.

Friends recommend silicol gel, made from natural colloidal silica. It works by neutralizing toxins and irritants found in rich food and alcohol, binding them and removing them safely from the gut. Take a tablespoon before drinking to protect the stomach and intestines.

WEIGH UP YOUR OPTIONS

Finally, before you go out, try thinking about just how fattening getting drunk can be. Do the math—you may be unpleasantly surprised. Say six alcoholic drinks, two cookies, and maybe four sugar-based drinks add up to about 2,000 calories. Does a young man or woman's social life improve as they become fat drunkards? No, it doesn't.

All in all, it's best to consider what to drink if you intend to drink a lot of it. Because beer is carbonated, for example, drinking it before liquor will allow your body to absorb the alcohol much more quickly, causing you to feel the effects faster than usual (hence the old adage "beer before whiskey, very risky"). Above all, don't mix your liquors. Your body takes longer to recognize and metabolize individual types.

Finally, before drinking, plan ahead. Leave a large bottle of water and a glass by the bed for when you return from a heavy night's drinking.

WHILE DRINKING

In addition to eating carbohydrates during any drinking session, remember to top up your non-alcoholic fluids, too. Water is especially important, as dehydration plays a big part in the hangover headache.

Go on the offensive by interspersing alcoholic drinks with water or water-based drinks. Drink a glass of water for every glass of wine or strong spirit. This slows down the number of drinks you have, and it also gives the kidneys and liver a break from alcohol. Try to avoid drinks laden with caffeine and acids, however. And as for carbonation: bubbly water is not recommended if you have a weak stomach.

Eating a few small snacks throughout the evening will help absorb alcohol, too.

Don't try to keep up with the boys. Women just don't have the inbuilt tolerance for alcohol that men do, even when they are the same size.

BEFORE RETIRING

As writer Jeffrey Bernard put it: "On retiring to the floor at night, the drinker should consume one or two pints of water if he or she can find the tap."

Wherever you end up, drink more water, from the tap or the bottle. The dehydration of drunkenness stimulates the body to absorb water from the brain, which shrinks it a bit, causing the headaches, dry mouth, and part of the general malaise of a hangover. By drinking water prior to sleep, you counteract dehydration, and speed up the elimination of alcohol from the body. If you are in a nauseous state, take small sips of still water at room temperature.

Ban caffeinated drinks, because coffee and the like only act to further dehydrate your body. Avoid acidic drinks, such as orange juice, if your stomach is upset. If you feel up to it, a glass of milk before bed helps protect the stomach from too much acid.

Eat more sugar, because alcohol breaks down sugar stored in the liver and that needs to be replaced. Some people recommend drinking energy drinks such as Gatorade before going to bed.

Try this one, which comes from Australia. The day before you know you might be getting drunk, go to the local supermarket and purchase a small watermelon. Get five Berroca (now available in the U.S.) tablets and dissolve them in a glass of water. Cut a small hole in the top of the melon. Pour the dissolved Berrocas inside the melon through the hole. Give the whole thing a gentle shake, and put in the refrigerator. Let it sit overnight, or while you're out getting legless. Spend the hangover day eating Berroca-soaked watermelon. It can't be that bad a tonic.

I have also heard that taking two aspirin before going to bed is good preventative action. Alas, our research revealed that it could make your hangover worse because it will increase the ratio of blood to alcohol in your body.

Taking painkillers the next day is not a good idea, either. They contain acid, which only unsettles your stomach more. Some painkillers also irritate the liver and can cause long-term damage, even bleeding, of the fragile stomach. Avoid anything containing acetominophen because it and alcohol do not mix well.

Forgive me for having to bring up this unpleasantness, but it has to be said. If you feel like throwing up, then get down on your knees and do it. Throwing up is good for your body because it gets rid of the toxins. The less alcohol inside you, the less severe your hangover will be. (The Romans, after all, retired to a vomitorium midway during a drinking session, relieved themselves, and returned to the party.) Remember, however, that vomiting will dehydrate you further and you should increase the amount of water or juice that you drink.

While all of this is good advice, in the end there is only one foolproof preventative: the words "No more."

HOW TO "CURE" A HANGOVER

DOGS' HAIRS AND OTHER TALES

In medieval times, if you were bitten by a dog, the village's medicine man used to clean out the wound and add a hair from the dog that had bitten you (if he could catch it). This is the basis of the legend of the "hair of the dog" as used in various hangover cures.

The hair-of-the-dog concept has remained popular in our drinking culture for centuries. Yet why do people recommend drinking more of the same stuff that made you feel ill in the first place? Adding more alcohol to a system already overwhelmed by it can only make matters worse, scientifically speaking.

Despite the title of this book, I'm here to tell you that it's a myth that if you drink more of exactly what you were drinking the night before—in particular the spirit you were drinking last—then you will be fine. Yet it is true that a much more moderate use of this principal will work wonders—which is why the restorative cocktails beginning on page 41 have been specially designed to give you some genuine relief, helped along by a small amount of alcohol to numb the pain.

For instance, if you were out drinking Champagne all night, having a Buck's Fizz at breakfast or brunch the next day will certainly buck you up, but in reality it's the vitamins in the fresh orange juice that help.

Similarly, downing a vodka-based Bloody Mary (see page 52), a favorite of millions of hangover sufferers, adds the beneficial effects of tomatoes, which contain loads of vitamin C and potassium. By the way, pure organic tomato juice is best to make this with, so read the label on a can or bottle closely to check out the ingredients.

DON'T TRY THESE AT HOME

Having debunked dogs' hairs in general, they still sound preferable to other options. In writing this book, I unearthed some incredible facts and came to the conclusion that past remedies for hangovers were, well, pretty scary. For instance, the Chinese placed a flat, round stone under the victim's tongue, which achieved the desired effect by making him or her sicker than they already were!

The Roman politician, Cato, was a great believer in a bowl of stewed cabbage topped with raw, bitter almonds. In the seventeenth century, one common European cure for overindulgence was flogging and bleeding, using leeches.

Mexicans didn't fare any better; a bowl of hominy, spices, tripe, and calf's feet was given to hangover sufferers. Puerto Ricans rubbed half a lemon under their armpits to wake up the body's system. Mongolians and Eskimos ate pickled sheep's eyes, sometimes with tomato juice, to cure a blinding headache.

Russians still drink salted, fizzy cabbage water, and the Germans are fond of sauerkraut juice, also made of cabbage, and stacked with vitamin C. The Scandinavians and the Dutch like raw herrings, salted and served with chopped, sweet-tasting onions. There is a logic behind it: sugar, salt to make you drink more water, and lots of sodium—but give me a Bloody Mary any day! Peruvians drink *mate de coca,* or coca-leaf tea, as a cure, which is a cleansing drink that also settles the stomach.

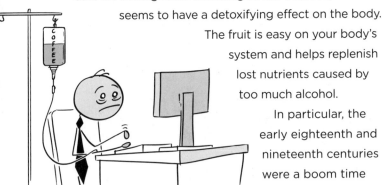

The liquid from a boiled banana is a traditional Chinese cure for a hangover. According to the Chinese, this seems to have a detoxifying effect on the body. The fruit is easy on your body's system and helps replenish lost nutrients caused by too much alcohol.

In particular, the early eighteenth and nineteenth centuries were a boom time for purveyors of hangover cures. Chemists dispensed potions with the magic words "guaranteed to cure a hangover" on their labels. Search the Internet today and you'll discover that the patent medicine industry is still thriving. The unsuspecting can be seduced into buying pills that will probably do no more than act as placebos.

COFFEE, TEA, OR FRIED FOOD?

In the seventeenth century, coffee was prized for its beneficial effect on the hangover, although even then, it had its detractors:

> In a word, coffee is the drunkard's settle-brain, the fool's pastime, who admires it for being the production of Asia, and is ravished with delight when he hears the berries grow in the deserts of Arabia, but would not give a farthing for a hogshead of it, if it were to be had on Hampstead Heath . . .
>
> —Thomas Tryon, *The Good House-Wife Made a Doctor*, 1692

It might seem to assist your body in waking up, but really, coffee is not a good thing to drink first thing in the morning. It doesn't sober you up because it doesn't decrease the amount of alcohol in the blood stream. Caffeine is a diuretic and will dehydrate you. Far better to stick to herbal brews such as peppermint and chamomile tea.

I have long considered the pros and cons of the classic greasy spoon breakfast the morning after. I can recall one ghastly experience early on in my marriage when my dear wife, Sue, feeling that I needed sustenance after a heavy drinking session the night before, approached the bedside carrying a tray with a plate of one foul and dark-looking sausage, two fried eggs ringed by fried bacon, and a deep orange pool of baked beans. I hid under the sumptuous bedcovers until she had taken it away. Sue now brings me my mother's recuperative recipe in the same situation (see page 76).

Imagine what grease does to your insides? Bacon causes acid to flow into the stomach and gives you indigestion. Sausages bring on a second acid attack. Fried eggs and fried bread make more pain for your stomach.

Eggs, though, loom large in hangover remedies and can be found in Egg Nog, the Prairie Oyster (see pages 67 and 110), and a Polish hangover cure of raw egg yolk, vodka, and a dash of black pepper; and, of course, scrambled eggs and smoked salmon.

Generally, though, it is far better to eat bland foods such as rice, apple sauce, and toast, either dry or with a little butter.

BACK TO BASICS

Really, the best thing to do, as I have said before, is to drink lots and lots of water. Yes, I know it is an effort, but if you can throw back dozens of Tequila shots and suck several lemons the night before, then you can drink six glasses of water at regular intervals over the next few hours. Add ice if you like, and a slice of lemon for extra fizz. Drinking water with bubbles is oxygenating as well as hydrating.

Finally, honey is underestimated as a useful ingredient in a hangover cure. Honey contains fructose, a fruit sugar that helps the body rid itself of alcohol, and helps balance the blood-sugar level—which, as you know by now, is low the morning after.

THE BLOODY MARY TRADITION

While the idea of "hair of the dog" is a myth in most cases, this is a cocktail known throughout the world for its restorative effects. There is no substitute for a Bloody Mary. Measure for measure, the curative factors combined in this drink are astonishing.

Harry's New York Bar (in Paris) is generally thought to be the birthplace of this cocktail. Paris in the 1920s was a second home to Americans in search of culture; among them was Ernest Hemingway, who held court at *Les Deux Magots* on the Left Bank of the Seine. The Bloody Mary year was 1921.

Fernand "Pete" Petiot combined tomato juice, vodka, salt, pepper, and Worcestershire sauce. There was nothing new about the vodka and tomato combination, but the addition of spices and the name were new. His inspiration was either

Mary Tudor, aka "Bloody Mary," or the actress Mary Pickford (accounts vary from author to author). Alas, Petiot is no longer with us to confirm precisely what he was thinking about at the time.

Vodka was available in Paris because Russian exiles from the 1917 revolution had brought their favorite drink with them. The arrival of canned tomato juice also made the cocktail's creation possible.

In 1934, America was introduced to the Bloody Mary after John Jacob Astor tasted it and convinced Petiot to travel to New York to work at the St. Regis Hotel. Astor insisted that Petiot rename it "Red Snapper" because he felt the word "bloody" was too rude for clients. Petiot used gin because vodka was not easily available in the U.S. at that time. When one customer, Prince Serge Obolensky, requested that his drink be "spiced up," Petiot obligingly added a dash of Tabasco sauce.

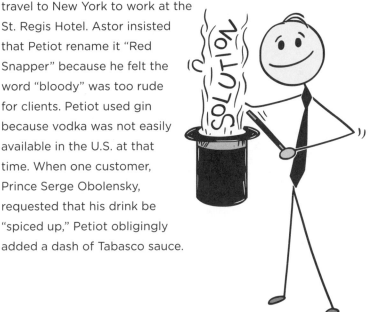

HAIR OF THE DOG
COCKTAILS

Here is my pick of the crop of restorative cocktails*, some made with less alcohol than usual so as not to overwhelm an already overloaded system. Unless otherwise stated, each makes one glass of liquid healing. All will soothe your ailing body. Trust me. I'm a bartender.

❋ ❋ ❋

*Some recipes contain raw egg. Consuming raw
egg may increase the risk of a food borne illness.*

AURA

A three-part whammy to revive you, starting at 7 am, with a quick breakfast hit of honey and milk.

2 OZ. (60ML) MILK

2 TABLESPOONS HONEY

Stir to boiling point in a saucepan. Pour into a mug and drink as hot as you can.

By 9 am you've reached the office. A bit of rum will cheer you up.

FRESHLY SQUEEZED JUICE OF ONE ORANGE

FRESHLY SQUEEZED JUICE OF HALF A LEMON

1 OZ. (30ML) LIGHT RUM

Stir to boiling point in a saucepan and pour into a heat-proof glass. Drink as hot as you can.

The final part of the Aura is your very own version of the 11 am morning coffee break. By this time, your eyes look more alert and a smile is beginning to play around your lips. You are ready to face the rest of the day.

1/2 OZ. (15ML) CAMPARI

1 OZ. (30ML) VODKA

3 OZ. (90ML) TOMATO JUICE

1/2 OZ. (15ML) FRESHLY SQUEEZED LEMON JUICE

3 DASHES WORCESTERSHIRE SAUCE

Pour all ingredients into a shaker filled with ice and shake. Strain into a highball filled with ice. Add a stick of celery, which you eat—it's good for you.

APOTHECARY COCKTAIL

This fantastic combination of herbal-based spirits is designed to restore your stomach to feeling the way it did before you went out. The very word "apothecary" conjures up the pharmacist's ability to dispense magical cures. Italian ingredients Punt e Mes and Fernet Branca combine with a creamy mint flavor to soothe the stomach.

1 OZ. (30ML) FERNET BRANCA

1 OZ. (30ML) WHITE CRÈME DE MENTHE

1 OZ. (30ML) PUNT E MES

Pour all ingredients into a mixing glass filled with ice. Stir. Strain into a cocktail glass.

BALTIMORE EGG NOG

A classic combination of a hair of the dog (brandy, dark rum, and Madeira) and soothing bulk (cream, egg, and milk). It's particularly good during the festive season.

1 OZ. (30ML) BRANDY

1 OZ. (30ML) MADEIRA

ABOUT 2/3 OZ. (20ML) DARK RUM

1 TABLESPOON SIMPLE SYRUP

1 FREE-RANGE EGG

ABOUT 2/3 OZ. (20ML) HEAVY CREAM

3 OZ. (90ML) MILK

Pour all ingredients into a shaker filled with ice. Shake. Strain into a highball glass filled with ice. Grate fresh nutmeg over the top.

BANANA COW

This recipe originally comes from Trader Vic's restaurant in Beverly Hills and was created by Chris Papajohn back in the 1960s. He believes it is the best hangover cure ever made—just like taking a cold shower. It can be made with or without alcohol, and served confidently.

1 OZ. (30ML) WHITE RUM

1 WHOLE, RIPE BANANA

3 OZ. (90ML) MILK

DASH ANGOSTURA BITTERS

DASH VANILLA ESSENCE

1 TEASPOON SUPERFINE (CASTOR) SUGAR

Pour all the ingredients into a blender and blend for ten seconds. Add half a scoop of crushed ice and blend again until smooth. Serve in a goblet.

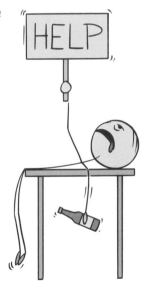

BARTENDER'S BREAKFAST

A cracking combination of herbs and spices designed to wake up the system. It's a good way to start the day; if you don't feel like eating breakfast, this will fill you up. The fresh ingredients, such as the tomato and herbs, will give you the vitamins you need to restore the spirit.

1 OZ. (30ML) VODKA

HANDFUL CHERRY TOMATOES

1 LEAF FRESH BASIL

PINCH GROUND CORIANDER

PINCH CELERY SALT

SPRINKLING CHOPPED CHIVES

PINCH CRACKED BLACK PEPPER

Pour all ingredients into a blender without ice. Blend until smooth. Strain into a highball glass filled with ice. Garnish with a cherry tomato and basil leaves on a cocktail stick—if you can muster the coordination!

BATONNET

My good friend Colin Peter Field, the bartender at Bar Hemingway in the Ritz Hotel, Paris, recommends this if a customer is lagging in energy. Cognac is always a great reviver, especially when it's combined with tonic.

1 OZ. (30ML) COGNAC

3 OZ. (90ML) WHITE WINE

TWO CINNAMON STICKS

TONIC WATER

Pour the Cognac and white wine into a tumbler filled with ice. Break the cinnamon sticks and drop them into the glass. Top up with tonic.

BLACK VELVET

Here's a heavy but delicious morning-after-the-night-before cocktail. The Guinness is full of iron, and is perfect combined with the sparkle of the Champagne. This drink was created to commemorate the death of Prince Albert in 1861, when England was in mourning. The bartender at the Brook's Club felt Champagne ought to be in mourning, too—and so combined it with Guinness.

1/2 GLASS CHILLED GUINNESS

1/2 GLASS CHILLED DRY CHAMPAGNE

Combine both ingredients in a tankard (like a stein). Sip slowly. Feel revived.

BLOOD TRANSFUSION

This deals with the stomach (through the Fernet Branca), then the headache, and finally the general malaise in the body. The combination will either cure you, or finish you off!

1 OZ. (30ML) VODKA

2/3 OZ. (20ML) SHERRY

1 OZ. (30ML) FERNET BRANCA

4 OZ. (120ML) TOMATO JUICE

1 OZ. (30ML) FRESH LIME JUICE

PINCH CELERY SALT

2 DASHES WORCESTERSHIRE SAUCE

Fill a highball glass with ice cubes. Pour the vodka and sherry over the ice first, then add the tomato and lime juice, then the celery salt and Worcestershire sauce. Stir. Float a layer of Fernet Branca on top.

BLOODY BULL

Known as the invincible hangover cure, this is an oldie but goodie. Based on the belief that beef makes the body stronger, it's a clever combination of two classic recipes: a Bullshot and a Bloody Mary. You end up with the best of both recipes.

1 OZ. (30ML) VODKA

2 OZ. (60ML) BEEF BOUILLON

2 OZ. (60ML) TOMATO JUICE

1 OZ. (30ML) FRESH LEMON JUICE

2 DASHES WORCESTERSHIRE SAUCE

PINCH CELERY SALT

Pour all ingredients into a cocktail shaker filled with ice. Shake. Strain into a highball glass filled with ice.

BLOODY CAESAR

This invigorating and restorative long drink was created for crooner Tony Bennett while he was performing a season in Las Vegas. On a night when he'd had one too many, he needed a quick reviver. The bartender at Caesars Palace came up with this mix. It worked.

1 OZ. (30ML) VODKA

4 OZ. (120ML) CLAMATO JUICE (A MIXTURE OF TOMATO AND CLAM JUICE)

ABOUT 2/3 OZ. (20ML) FRESH LEMON JUICE

PINCH CELERY SALT

DASH TABASCO SAUCE

2 DASHES WORCESTERSHIRE SAUCE

FRESHLY GROUND BLACK PEPPER

Pour the Clamato and lemon juices into a highball glass filled with ice. Add the vodka and other ingredients. Stir. Garnish with a wedge of lime on the rim. Serve with a stirrer.

BLOODY MARIA

This recipe is actually a Bloody Mary made with silver Tequila—
great when you had too many Margaritas the night before.

1 OZ. (30ML) SILVER TEQUILA

4 OZ. (120ML) TOMATO JUICE

DASH FRESH LEMON JUICE

PINCH CELERY SALT

PINCH BLACK PEPPER

4 DASHES TABASCO SAUCE

4 DASHES WORCESTERSHIRE SAUCE

Pour all ingredients into a cocktail shaker filled with ice.
Shake. Strain into a highball glass filled with ice. Garnish
with a celery stick and a wedge of lime.

BLOODY MARY

For the history behind this classic, see pages 38–39. Some brands of tomato juice contain spices, but they're not always listed. Best to add your own to make the Bloody Mary your body knows and loves.

1 OZ. (30ML) VODKA

4 OZ. (120ML) TOMATO JUICE

ABOUT 2/3 FL. OZ. (20ML) FRESH LEMON JUICE

PINCH CELERY SALT

2 DASHES WORCESTERSHIRE SAUCE

2 DASHES TABASCO SAUCE

FRESHLY GROUND BLACK PEPPER

CELERY STALK (OPTIONAL)

Fill a highball glass with ice cubes, then pour in the tomato and lemon juices. Add the vodka. Add the other items and stir. Add a quick grinding of black pepper. Garnish with a wedge of lime on the rim, and a stalk of celery if requested. Serve with a stirrer.

BLOODY SWEDISH BLONDE

A remedy for those who cannot face eating a pickled herring with schnapps first thing in the morning. Fennel is helpful in calming the nerves, as well as being full of minerals and high in calcium.

1 OZ. (30ML) AQUAVIT

ABOUT 4 OZ. (120ML) TOMATO JUICE

PINCH GROUND TOASTED FENNEL SEED

ABOUT 2/3 OZ. (20ML) FRESH LEMON JUICE

LARGE PINCH CARAWAY SEED

LEMON TWIST

SALT AND PEPPER, TO TASTE

Combine the aquavit, tomato juice, and ground fennel in a mixing glass and swirl it around gently. Strain into a highball glass filled with ice cubes. Add the lemon juice. Garnish with caraway seeds and a twist of lemon. Serve with a stirrer.

BODY & SOUL REVIVER

The name of this cocktail says it all. Both spirit ingredients are restorative, and the orange bitters is medicinal, too.

1 OZ. (30ML) BRANCA MENTHE

1 OZ. (30ML) COGNAC

DASH ORANGE BITTERS

Pour all ingredients into a cocktail shaker filled with ice. Shake. Strain into a shot glass.

BOSTON FLIP

The flip was traditionally made by flipping the combination between two containers to obtain a smooth consistency. During the seventeenth century, a flip featured beaten eggs, sugar, spices, rum, and hot ale. The innkeeper would mull the mixture with a hot iron "loggerhead" (poker) before serving it. The cocktail has changed dramatically since then. It is now a short drink, served cold with a sprinkling of nutmeg. It can be made with any spirit.

1 OZ. (30ML) BOURBON

1 OZ. (30ML) MADEIRA

1 FREE-RANGE EGG YOLK

DASH SIMPLE SYRUP

Pour all ingredients into a cocktail shaker filled with ice. Shake well. Strain into a goblet. Garnish with grated nutmeg.

BOURBON PICK-ME-UP

The combination of the earthiness of the bourbon and the fresh mint, combined with the aroma of the Branca Menthe, makes this one a sure-fire solution to a hangover. It's especially good for bourbon lovers who drank too much of it the night before. This really wakes up the system, helps the digestion, and the citrus-fruit/mint flavor cleanses your mouth, leaving it fresh and kissable.

1 OZ. (30ML) BOURBON

ABOUT 2/3 OZ. (20ML) BRANCA MENTHE

ABOUT 2/3 OZ. (20ML) FRESH LEMON JUICE

8 FRESH MINT LEAVES

Pour all ingredients into a cocktail shaker filled with ice. Shake. Strain into an old-fashioned glass filled with ice. Garnish with a sprig of fresh mint.

BRANDY FLIP

Flips are in the same family as egg flogs. They contain the yolk of a fresh egg but never milk. They can be made with any of the following spirits: gin, whisky, brandy, rum, port, sherry, or claret. Serve in a regular wine glass. This brandy recipe has lots of sugar to balance blood-sugar levels, as well as brandy to liven you up.

1 OZ. (30ML) BRANDY

1 WHOLE FREE-RANGE EGG

2 TEASPOONS SUPERFINE (CASTOR) SUGAR

Pour all ingredients into a cocktail shaker filled with ice. Shake and strain into a wine glass. Grate fresh nutmeg over the top.

BREAKFAST EGG NOG

Eggs are rich in the amino acid cysteine, high in protein, and they aid the liver in producing glutathione. Eggs and milk are a soothing combination, and also help provide energy. Brandy gives you a kick, and the Curaçao gives you just the sweetness you need.

1 FRESH FREE-RANGE EGG

1 OZ. (30ML) ORANGE CURAÇAO

1 OZ. (30ML) BRANDY

5 OZ. (150ML) MILK

Pour all ingredients, except the milk, into a cocktail shaker filled with ice. Shake. Strain into a highball glass and add the milk. Stir. Sprinkle freshly grated nutmeg over the top.

BROKEN SPUR COCKTAIL

If you've overindulged and are facing a day on horseback and can't get out of it, try one of these. Remember not to spur the horse too hard—it's not his fault!

ABOUT 2/3 OZ. (20ML) GIN

ABOUT 2/3 OZ. (20ML) ITALIAN VERMOUTH

1-1/2 OZ. (40ML) WHITE PORT

1 TEASPOON ANISETTE

Pour all the ingredients into a cocktail shaker filled with ice. Shake. Strain into a cocktail glass.

. . . .

BUCK'S FIZZ

Mr. McGarry, a bartender at the Buck's Club, London, created this delicious combination in 1921. His recipe is specific about the ratio of two-thirds Champagne to one-third fresh orange juice. This is good for anyone who drank too much Champagne the night before. It's the hair of one very sophisticated dog!

FRESH ORANGE JUICE

CHAMPAGNE

The size of the Champagne glass dictates how much of the above you will use. Follow his two-thirds Champagne to one-third orange juice, and stir gently.

BULLDOG

A little bit of alcohol, a sour citrus, and the spicy heat of a pepper to awaken the senses, calm the stomach and, hopefully, give you a little boost in your day.

1 OZ. (30ML) GIN

1/2 OZ. (15ML) FRESH LEMON JUICE

1 TEASPOON HONEY

2 OR 3 DASHES RED TABASCO

Pour all the ingredients into a shaker filled with ice, shake, and strain into a small glass. For an extra kick, add a slice of fresh chilli to the drink.

BULLSHOT

A classic, nutritious, and invigorating drink that can replace lunch if you don't feel like real food. Its name was inspired by the beef bouillon ingredient. Protein from the beef is balanced by all the other flavors. The kick comes from the Tabasco and Worcestershire.

1 OZ. (30ML) VODKA

4 OZ. (120ML) BEEF BOUILLON

DASH FRESH LEMON JUICE

2 DASHES WORCESTERSHIRE SAUCE

CELERY SALT

TABASCO SAUCE

FRESHLY GROUND BLACK PEPPER

Pour the bouillon, lemon juice, Tabasco, and Worcestershire sauces into a cocktail shaker filled with ice, along with the vodka. Shake. Strain into an old-fashioned glass with ice. Add a quick grinding of black pepper. Garnish with a wedge of lime on the rim. Serve with a stirrer.

CAMPARI NOBILE

An award-winner I created for the 1993 Campari Barman of the Year competition. The juices are full of vitamins, and the bitter lemon is refreshing. Limoncello, from Italy's Amalfi coast, adds sunshine to your spirits.

ABOUT 2/3 OZ. (20ML) VODKA

ABOUT 2/3 OZ. (20ML) CAMPARI

1/3 OZ. (10ML) LIMONCELLO

3 OZ. (90ML) COMBINED FRESH ORANGE AND RASPBERRY JUICES

BITTER LEMON

Pour all ingredients, except the bitter lemon, into a cocktail shaker filled with ice. Shake. Strain into a highball glass filled with ice. Top up with bitter lemon. Stir. Garnish with five raspberries and a sprig of mint, plus a twist of orange on the rim. Serve with a stirrer.

CECIL PICK-ME-UP

A pre-Prohibition recipe with three essential pick-me-up ingredients: Champagne, egg, and brandy. Who was Cecil? A mystery man, he must have been well known for being hungover to have a cocktail named after him.

1 FREE-RANGE EGG YOLK

1 OZ. (30ML) BRANDY

1 TEASPOON SUPERFINE (CASTOR) SUGAR

CHAMPAGNE

Pour all the ingredients, except for the Champagne, into a cocktail shaker filled with ice. Shake. Strain into a Champagne flute. Top up with Champagne.

CHAMPAGNE COCKTAIL

The origins of this cocktail are shrouded in mystery, but it is believed to have come from the southern states of America. Whatever its roots, it remains a classic—and it's unlikely anyone will refuse it, if offered.

CHAMPAGNE

COGNAC

1 SUGAR CUBE

ANGOSTURA BITTERS

SLICES OF ORANGE

Place a cube of sugar in each Champagne flute and soak with the Angostura bitters. Add enough Cognac to cover the sugar cube and fill the glasses with Champagne. Garnish with slices of orange.

CHAMPAGNE PICK-ME-UP

A flavorful combination for Champagne lovers. The citric ingredients will certainly help buck you up after a night on the town—and the vitamins they contain will help you get back on an even keel.

1 OZ. (30ML) BRANDY

ABOUT 2/3 OZ. (20ML) FRESH ORANGE JUICE

ABOUT 2/3 OZ. (20ML) FRESH LEMON JUICE

CHAMPAGNE

Pour the first three ingredients into a cocktail shaker filled with ice. Shake. Strain into a Champagne flute. Stir. Top up with Champagne. Stir.

CORPSE REVIVERS

Bars tend to be piled with corpses after a heavy night's drinking. The bodies are there, but the souls are missing. They need reviving; that's why they're in the bar—back where it all started. Fortunately, every good barman knows the curative effect one of these can have upon a departed soul.

VERSION 1

Created circa 1926 by Frank Meier at the Cambon Bar, The Ritz, Paris.

1 GLASS PERNOD

JUICE OF A QUARTER LEMON

CHAMPAGNE

Pour the lemon juice and Pernod into a Champagne coupe over a cube of ice. Fill with Champagne. Stir slowly. Serve.

VERSION 2

From *The Savoy Cocktail Book* (1930) and still popular in nearly every bar in the world.

1/2 OZ. (15ML) BRANDY

1/2 OZ. (15ML) SWEET VERMOUTH

1/2 OZ. (15ML) CALVADOS

Pour all ingredients into a mixing glass filled with ice. Stir. Strain into a cocktail glass.

VERSION 3

Created in 1948 by Johnny Johnson at the Savoy's American Bar in London.

1/2 OZ. (15ML) BRANDY

1/2 OZ. (15ML) WHITE CRÈME DE MENTHE

1/2 OZ. (15ML) FERNET BRANCA

Pour all ingredients into a mixing glass filled with ice. Stir. Strain into a cocktail glass.

DRUGSTORE

Here's a medicinal cocktail with a touch of sweetness from the wine-based vermouth. It is quite refreshing, and very good for the digestive system.

1 OZ. (30ML) FERNET BRANCA

1/2 OZ. (15ML) SWEET VERMOUTH

1/2 OZ. (15ML) WHITE CRÈME DE MENTHE

Pour all ingredients into a mixing glass filled with ice. Stir well. Strain into a liqueur glass.

EGG NOG

This is the traditional, Christmas morning egg nog recipe. Its origins are unclear, but the name could date from the seventeenth-century English habit of adding a beaten egg to a "noggin"—a small mug of strong beer. You can thicken the mixture by adding more egg yolk, or thin it by adding more milk.

1 FREE-RANGE EGG

1 OZ. (30ML) BRANDY

1 OZ. (30ML) DARK RUM

3 OZ. (90ML) MILK

1 TBSP SIMPLE SYRUP

Pour all ingredients, except the milk, into a cocktail shaker. Shake. Strain into a goblet. Stir in the milk. Grate fresh nutmeg on top.

EYE-OPENER COCKTAIL

This is an old recipe and will certainly open your eyes wide in an instant. Absinthe makes the eyelids stronger; don't have too many, though, or they'll remain open permanently.

2 DASHES ABSINTHE

2 DASHES ORANGE CURAÇAO

2 DASHES CRÈME DE NOYAU

1 OZ. (30ML) RUM

1 TEASPOON SUPERFINE (CASTOR) SUGAR

1 FREE-RANGE EGG YOLK

Pour all the ingredients into a cocktail shaker filled with ice. Shake. Strain into a cocktail glass.

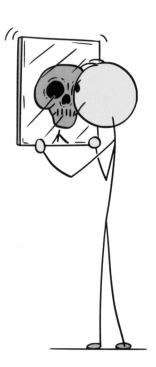

FALLEN ANGEL

A classic gin-based cocktail to be taken after a restless night searching for the angel who was by your side and seems to have disappeared at dawn.

1-1/2 OZ. (45ML) GIN

DASH WHITE CRÈME DE MENTHE

DASH ANGOSTURA BITTERS

DASH FRESH LEMON JUICE

Pour into a cocktail shaker filled with ice. Shake well. Strain into a cocktail glass.

FERNET BRANCA COCKTAIL

One of the best morning-after cocktails ever invented. Fernet Branca is an Italian bitters made from over forty herbs distilled in grape alcohol that has been produced since 1844 by the Branca family. The herbs include: aloe vera, which purifies the blood and cleanses the liver; angelica, which stimulates digestion; chamomile, which calms nerves and muscles; cinchona, the source of quinine, used to treat digestive disorders and fevers; gentian, which stimulates the appetite; peppermint, effective against nausea and heartburn; and finally, saffron, rue, and wormwood.

1 OZ. (30ML) FERNET BRANCA

1 OZ. (30ML) SWEET VERMOUTH

1 OZ. (30ML) GIN

Pour all ingredients into a cocktail shaker filled with ice. Shake. Strain into a cocktail glass.

GERETY'S REMEDY

This is from an Irishman, the late father of a very good friend who enjoyed a drink or two. He guaranteed that you would feel better after this dark and potent concoction. It's full of vitamins and iron. If you think two eggs are a little too much for you, use only one.

10 OZ. (300ML) OF GUINNESS

5 OZ. (150ML) MILK

2 FREE-RANGE EGGS

SALT AND PEPPER

GRATED NUTMEG

Beat the eggs with a pinch of salt and pepper, pour on the milk, add a pinch of nutmeg, and give it a good stir. Pour the mixture into a pint glass, top up with the Guinness, and stir well.

HAIR OF THE DOG

According to *The Jeeves Cocktail Book*, this is what Jeeves used to serve in the morning to his befuddled master, Bertie Wooster. The honey will stay in your system longer than straight sugar. Also, it's purer and contains helpful trace minerals.

1-1/2 OZ. (45ML) SCOTCH

1 OZ. (30ML) DOUBLE CREAM

LARGE TEASPOON CLEAR HONEY

Pour all ingredients into a cocktail shaker filled with ice. Shake vigorously to let the honey infuse. Strain into a cocktail glass. Serve.

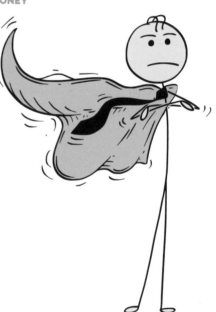

HARRY'S PICK-ME-UP

Grenadine, which is a pomegranate syrup, adds an exotic touch to this pick-me-up-while-I-am-down-in-the-dumps cocktail.

1 OZ. (30ML) BRANDY

1 TEASPOON GRENADINE

JUICE OF HALF A LEMON

CHAMPAGNE

Shake all ingredients, except the Champagne, in a cocktail shaker filled with ice. Strain into a Champagne flute, then top up with Champagne and serve.

. . . .

PORT FLIP

Here's a recipe that my friend Dale DeGroff recommends for when you want the night to continue until dawn. It's very hair-of-the-dog material, but effective—and it's a pretty color, too.

1-1/2 OZ. (45ML) RUBY PORT

1 OZ. (30ML) BRANDY

1 FREE-RANGE EGG YOLK

Pour all the ingredients into a cocktail shaker filled with ice. Shake. Strain into a small wine glass. Garnish with a dusting of freshly grated nutmeg.

RED SNAPPER

This is the recipe for a Bloody Mary made with gin, not vodka. Parisian Fernand Petiot, who worked at the King Cole Bar in New York's St. Regis Hotel, made this at John Jacob Astor's request.

1 OZ. (30ML) GIN

4 OZ. (120ML) TOMATO JUICE

DASH FRESH LEMON JUICE

PINCH CELERY SALT

2 DASHES WORCESTERSHIRE SAUCE

2 DASHES TABASCO SAUCE

FRESHLY GROUND BLACK PEPPER

Fill a highball glass with ice cubes, then pour in the tomato and lemon juices. Add the gin. Add the spices and stir. Add a quick twist of black pepper. Garnish with a wedge of lime on the rim, and a stalk of celery, if requested. Serve with a stirrer.

RITZ REVIVER

If you wake up in Paris with an elegant hangover induced by too much vintage Champagne, head for the Ritz Bar and have one of these to re-energize your soul.

1 OZ. (30ML) FERNET BRANCA

1 OZ. (30ML) CRÈME DE MENTHE

DASH ANGOSTURA BITTERS

TWIST OF ORANGE PEEL

Rub the rim of a cocktail glass with the orange peel. Shake all the ingredients in a cocktail shaker filled with ice. Strain into a cocktail glass. Drop in the twist of orange peel, and serve.

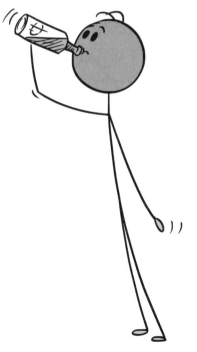

ROSA'S MAGICAL CURE

This is the concoction my mother used to make when she saw I needed revitalizing, and it was my first encounter with a hangover cure. I remember the sensation of many layers of flavors, ranging from the sweetness of Marsala, sharpness of lemon juice, the spice of chili, and the egg that binds it together.

1 FREE-RANGE EGG YOLK

PINCH GROUND CHILI PEPPER

1 SMALL TEASPOON FRESH LEMON JUICE

1 OZ. (30ML) SWEET MARSALA

Separate the yolk from the egg white and discard the latter. Place the yolk, without breaking it, in a small glass. Add the ground chili, the lemon juice, then the Marsala. Don't stir it. Drink it all down in one gulp. Serve with a freshly made zabaglione to follow—this gives you even more energy.

SALVAMENTO!

This is an old recipe invented by Horacio Tamayo, a bartender from Mexico City. The word *salvamento* means "lifesaving"—so appropriate in this situation.

1 EGG, BEATEN

JUICE OF ONE LEMON

1 TEASPOON SUGAR

1 OZ. (30ML) GIN

SODA WATER

Pour all the ingredients, except the soda water, into a cocktail shaker filled with ice. Shake well. Strain into a highball glass filled with ice and top up with soda.

SPIRIT LIFTER

I like this combination of bittersweet citric flavors—perhaps because I love Campari. This little cocktail will work very well on a chihuahua-sized hangover.

1 OZ. (30ML) COINTREAU

1 OZ. (30ML) CAMPARI

1 OZ. (30ML) FRESH ORANGE JUICE

Pour all ingredients into a cocktail shaker filled with ice. Strain into chilled cocktail glasses and serve.

STOMACH REVIVER

An excellent recipe for an upset stomach, and Fernet Branca's medicinal qualities will help calm your nerves. Drink this slightly bitter-tasting cocktail down in one gulp and you'll feel much better.

1 OZ. (30ML) FERNET BRANCA

1 OZ. (30ML) BRANDY

3 DASHES ANGOSTURA BITTERS

Pour all ingredients into a cocktail shaker filled with ice. Shake. Strain into a shot glass, then knock it back and breath a sigh of relief.

SUFFERING BASTARD

An apt name for the state you'll find yourself in when you need this cocktail. Whatever your poison the night before, the ginger ale in this will be good for you. Trust me.

ANGOSTURA BITTERS

1/2 OZ. (15ML) GIN

I/2 OZ. (15ML) BRANDY

1 TEASPOON LIME JUICE

COLD GINGER ALE

Swirl the Angostura bitters around a highball glass and toss away the excess. Half fill the glass with ice and add the gin, brandy, lime juice, and ginger ale. Stir. Garnish with slices of lime, cucumber, and orange. Add a sprig of mint.

SURF AND TURF

This dream of a recipe is for more than one person. Prepare this the day before for your guests to drink the morning after; you may not be capable of doing it in the next day. It's liquid brunch.

Serves 6:

6 OZ. (180ML) VODKA

15 OZ. (450ML) TOMATO JUICE

4 TEASPOONS FRESH
    LEMON JUICE

4 OZ. (120ML) CLAM JUICE

1/2 OZ. (15ML) STEAK SAUCE OR
    BROWN SAUCE

2 TEASPOONS FRESHLY GROUND
    BLACK PEPPER

4 DASHES CELERY SALT

4 DASHES HOT CHILI SAUCE

Garnishes:

CHILLED LOBSTER TAILS
    (COOKED)

FILET MIGNON CUBES
    GRILLED (BROILED)

SPRING ONIONS
    (SCALLIONS)

Combine the vodka, tomato, lemon, clam juices, and steak sauce in a jug or pitcher and stir well. Add the pepper, the celery salt, and hot chili sauce to taste. Fill wide-brimmed highball glasses with ice cubes and pour the mixture to three-quarters full. Garnish with a lobster tail and a piece of grilled beef on a single skewer. Trim the spring onion and add to the glass. Serve. Watch guests come alive.

TOKYO BLOODY MARY

Specially designed for those suffering from a sake hangover. It's basically a Bloody Mary with sake.

1 OZ. (30ML) SAKE

4 OZ. (120ML) TOMATO JUICE

ABOUT 2/3 OZ. (20ML) FRESH LEMON JUICE

8 DASHES TABASCO SAUCE

4 DASHES WORCESTERSHIRE SAUCE

4 DASHES MEDIUM SHERRY

1 PINCH CELERY SALT

1 PINCH BLACK PEPPER

Pour all the ingredients into cocktail shaker filled with ice. Shake. Strain into a highball glass filled with ice. Garnish with a stick of celery. Serve.

VAMPIRO

The national drink of Mexico. It's a strange combination of orange and tomato juice, spices, honey, and onion (yes, really)—but it creates a drink full of flavor. Make it the day before and leave in the fridge overnight.

ABOUT 2-1/2 OZ. (75ML) TOMATO JUICE

I OZ. (30ML) FRESH ORANGE JUICE

I OZ. (30ML) SILVER TEQUILA

1 TEASPOON CLEAR HONEY

ABOUT 1/3 OZ. (10ML) FRESH LIME JUICE

HALF A SLICE OF ONION, FINELY CHOPPED

A FEW SLICES FRESH RED-HOT CHILI

A FEW DROPS WORCESTERSHIRE SAUCE

SALT, TO TASTE

Pour all the ingredients into a cocktail shaker filled with ice. Shake well to release the flavors. Strain into a highball glass filled with ice. Garnish with a wedge of lime on the rim.

WAKE-UP CALL

I created this for New Year's Day after the millennium. Tomato juice and Champagne you ask? Trust me, it works. Lemon juice is good for the liver. The Tabasco sauce? Well, it just tastes good in this combination.

1 OZ. (30ML) VODKA

ABOUT 2/3 OZ. (20ML) COINTREAU

ABOUT 1/3 OZ. (10ML) FRESH LEMON JUICE

3 OZ. (90ML) TOMATO JUICE

CHAMPAGNE

TABASCO SAUCE

PINCH CELERY SALT

PINCH SUPERFINE (CASTOR) SUGAR

Pour all the ingredients, with the exception of the Champagne, into a shaker filled with ice. Shake. Pour into a highball glass filled with ice to about three-quarters full. Top up with Champagne. Stir. Garnish with a wedge of lime.

007 REVIVER

Brunch in a glass with a hit of vitality.

Serves 6:

10 OZ. (300ML) VODKA

4 MEDIUM CELERY STALKS

2 MEDIUM CARROTS

1 LARGE RED PEPPER, SEEDS REMOVED

1 LARGE GREEN PEPPER, SEEDS REMOVED

1/4 ONION, CHOPPED

20 OZ. (600ML) BOTTLED TOMATO JUICE

1 TABLESPOON HOT PEPPER SAUCE

1 TEASPOON FRESHLY GROUND BLACK PEPPER

1 TEASPOON SALT

LEMON WEDGES

Juice each vegetable separately and combine in a large jug.
Add the tomato juice, hot sauce, black pepper, and salt.
Stir well. Place in the fridge to chill. To serve, pour 1-1/2 oz.
(45ml) vodka into a highball glass filled with ice. Add the
vegetable mix and a wedge of lemon. Stir.

NON-ALCOHOLIC REMEDIES

 ll of these recipes are nutritious and work in different ways to help the body recover.

THE RIGHT STUFF

The non-alcoholic recipes in this section are viewed as energy sources. Jugs of healthy, fruit-, or vegetable-based drinks will give you vitamins, antioxidants, and other beneficial alkalines to help recover your energy. Anyone can prepare and enjoy juices, either as cool, refreshing liquids or as smoothies, using ingredients such as yogurt or soy milk, tofu, and rice milk: all important sources of protein.

Generally, you can combine fruit with fruit, but you can also combine vegetables and fruit, if you like the taste. Experiment to see which vegetables and fruits help you most.

Personally, I prefer to eat good things from the fruit bowl: bananas, pears, oranges, pineapple, melons, papayas, blueberries, blackcurrants, and cranberries. They're full of vitamins, antioxidants, minerals, and other nutrients. All antioxidants are your friends. These are a group of nutrients found in fruit and vegetables and include vitamins C, E, and A, and betacarotene. They attack oxygen molecules known as free radicals that damage healthy blood cells and are known to be a cause of hardening of the arteries.

Choose your juicer with care; whichever design you decide on, remember that you're going to have to clean it. Juicers aren't that expensive, but be sure to buy one that really does

extract juice and has a solid blade that will last more than a few months.

CHOOSING FRUIT

Select only the best quality you can afford—preferably organic. Wash and dry any fruit with a skin. Wash fragile berries such as raspberries, blueberries, blackberries, and fresh cranberries in a sieve and leave to drain on a paper towel.

You can prepare many fruits for juicing in advance, which can be a real life-saver the morning after. The following is a short guide to preparing fruit for juicing.

Apples: Peel, core, and halve.

Bananas: Peel.

Canteloupe: Slice off both ends. Place one end on the cutting board. Make a slice from top to bottom and remove the rind. Halve. Remove the seeds. Dice.

Grapes: Choose seedless grapes for juicing. Wash and leave to drain on a paper towel.

Grapefruit, Lemons, Limes, Oranges: Peel and cut into segments.

Kiwi Fruit: Peel, then dice the flesh.

Mangoes: Peel; slice the fruit away from the central seed.

Papayas: Halve, remove the seeds with a teaspoon. Peel and dice the flesh.

Passion Fruit: Halve and scoop out the fruit. Place in a

strainer to remove the hard seeds, or use as is—the seeds are not harmful.

Peaches: Peel, halve, remove the stone, and dice.

Pears: Peel, core, and dice.

Pineapples: Slice off the top and bottom. Cut from top to bottom to remove all of the rough skin. Cut into halves and cut away the hard center core.

Strawberries: Hull with a sharp knife or one of those cute hull-removers. Cut in half.

WHICH VEGETABLES?

Another good thing for a hangover is to eat raw or grated carrots, or drink them juiced. When I hear my wife Sue press the juicer button, I know recovery will be mine once I have tasted whatever combination of vegetable juices she has decided on for me.

She is absolutely right, because vegetables such as carrots support the liver, and are invaluable as a detoxifier. They're rich in carotene, which is converted to vitamin A by the liver.

If you're not into carrots, then choose from any of the following: avocados, broccoli, Brussels sprouts, cabbage, cauliflower, lettuce, parsley, pumpkin and other squashes, tomatoes, and spinach.

Green and sprout vegetable juices, broccoli, asparagus, and many herbs contain the vitamin B complex, which is good for helping you to recover. In fact, God's gift to hangovers is vitamin B1 (thiamine). It calms your shaky nervous system, helps your weary body break down any alcohol that's decided to hang around. Good sources are asparagus, herbs, beans, rice, grains, cereal, and nuts.

The alkaline content in a vegetable such as celery balances the acidity in your troubled stomach. Make lots of celery juice or add celery juice to your favorite juicy drink.

For fatigue, try juicing alfalfa sprouts, artichokes, bean sprouts, and spinach. When you cook spinach, save the water from it and add this to a combination for more health.

Drink pure fresh tomato juice or V8, which comes in a handy-sized can. The latter is full of vitamins B, C, lycopene, plus hints of spinach, beetroot, watercress, lettuce, parsley, celery, carrot, and tomato.

Vitamin E is brilliant because it helps the heart function. It's found in fresh beetroot, green juices, whole grains, and nuts.

ALLEGRIA

The name means "happiness" in Italian. This drink is refreshing—
and it contains only seventy-eight calories.

1/2 RIPE MANGO, PEELED, CUT, AND DICED

2 OZ. (60ML) CARROT JUICE

2 OZ. (60ML) PINEAPPLE JUICE

2 OZ. (60ML) FRESH ORANGE JUICE

ABOUT 2/3 OZ. (20ML) FRESH LEMON JUICE

STILL MINERAL WATER

Put the mango pieces in a blender and add
all other ingredients except the water and
a scoop of crushed ice. Blend. Pour
the mixture into a large glass. Fill to
three-quarters full. Add the water
to dilute the mixture a little. Stir.

AUNT EMMA'S
HANGOVER COCKTAIL

The spices, onion, and celery (a diuretic) are all good for your hungover body.

- 5 OZ. (150ML) TOMATO JUICE
- 3 TABLESPOONS VINEGAR
- JUICE OF 1 LEMON
- 4 SLICES OF ONION
- 3 TABLESPOONS SUGAR
- 4 CELERY STALKS
- 2 TEASPOONS RED TABASCO
- SALT AND PEPPER, TO TASTE

Juice the lemon and chop the celery into small pieces. Mix all of the ingredients in a container and let stand overnight in the refrigerator. Strain and serve in a glass.

BANANA AND STRAWBERRY SMOOTHIE

This is brilliant if you're planning a night's drinking. Mix this before you go and you'll be fine (hopefully). The yogurt will line and protect your stomach from acidic onslaught.

1 LARGE RIPE BANANA

3 TABLESPOONS PLAIN NATURAL YOGURT

6 FRESH STRAWBERRIES

ICE CUBES

Peel the banana and break it into pieces. Wash and hull the strawberries and slice them in half. Put everything in a blender, and blend until smooth. Serve over ice in a tall glass.

BERRY NICE

Blueberries are packed with vitamin A and potassium, as are pears. And the orange juice and blackcurrants give you plenty of vitamin C.

1 CUP BLUEBERRIES, FRESH OR FROZEN

1 CUP BLACKCURRANTS

2 PEARS

JUICE OF 1 ORANGE

Wash the fruit. Squeeze the orange juice and add it to the blender along with the fruit. Blend until smooth. Serve over ice in a tumbler.

BLOOD-SUGAR TONIC

Valuable minerals and a whole range of vitamins are found in the alfalfa sprouts. You'll love the kick this gives you. Fennel adds an aniseed flavor.

- 8 OZ. (225G) ALFALFA SPROUTS
- 8 OZ. (225G). MUNG SPROUTS
- 8 OZ. (225G) LENTIL SPROUTS
- 2 KALE LEAVES
- 8 OZ. (225G) JERUSALEM ARTICHOKES
- 1 HANDFUL STRING BEANS
- 1 MEDIUM PARSNIP
- 4 OZ. (115G) CUP FENNEL

Wash all the vegetables and push them through a juicer or blender. Serve over ice.

BOING-BOING

You'll get lots of bounce from this energy-giving drink. The honey deals with the alcohol, while the yogurt soothes your stomach. The sugars from the banana help to cheer you up.

1/2 RIPE BANANA

1 TEASPOON CLEAR HONEY

2 TEASPOON YOGURT WATER
(THE LIQUID ON TOP OF YOUR YOGURT)

Place all ingredients into a blender and blend until smooth. Add a little water in the blender if you prefer a longer drink. Pour into a highball glass filled with ice.

BREATH ENHANCER

For when your breath just isn't kissable. Parsley is also good as a blood cleanser. Carrots make this high in vitamin A.

JUICE OF 1 ORANGE

4 MEDIUM CARROTS

1 TEASPOON SUPERFINE (CASTOR) SUGAR

4 LARGE SPRIGS PARSLEY

Cut the orange in half and squeeze. Pour into a glass. Juice the carrots with the sprigs of parsley at the same time. Add to the orange juice with the teaspoon of sugar and stir. Drink quickly.

CLEANSER COCKTAIL

The papaya and melon will get your energy going. It's good to prepare this the day before you know you're going to need it—for instance, if you're going to a party or a wedding.

Serves 4:

1/2 YELLOW MELON

1/2 PAPAYA

1/2 MANGO

6 STRAWBERRIES

10 OZ. (300ML) PASSION FRUIT JUICE

10 OZ. (300ML) PEACH JUICE

1 OZ. (30ML) GRENADINE

JUICE OF 1 LEMON

JUICE OF 1 ORANGE

Peel the fruit and dice. Place all ingredients in a blender and blend until smooth. Pour in a jug and leave until you need it. To make it less bulky, add a dash of still mineral water.

DALE DEGROFF'S
MACHO GAZPACHO

Dale, legendary bartender of New York City's famous Rainbow Room for many years, once asked the chef there for a hangover cure. The chef suggested using various vegetables strained through a chinois (a fine-mesh strainer)—which is the reason this cocktail is full of vitamins. This recipe will yield about 3-1/2 quarts, so you can keep it for days in the fridge, for when friends have stayed over after a hard night's drinking.

6 LARGE CUCUMBERS

4 RED ONIONS

1 JALAPEÑO PEPPER, SPLIT

2 BUNCHES SPRING ONIONS

8 GREEN BELL PEPPERS

6 STICKS CELERY, CUT INTO
   1-INCH (3 CM) PIECES

BUNCH WATERCRESS

SALT AND PEPPER, TO TASTE

FRESH LEMON AND LIME JUICE, TO TASTE

Combine small batches of vegetables in a food processor and purée. When all have been processed, place the purée in a container and cover with three liters (about three quarts) of water. Place in the refrigerator for about an hour. Stir the mixture and strain using a fine strainer. Adjust the seasoning and add lime and lemon juices to taste. Serve with or without ice.

GINGER ALERT

A drink designed to give your system a wake-up call. A great fusion of juice and ginger flavor.

3 OZ. (90ML) APPLE JUICE

2 OZ. (60ML) PEAR JUICE

JUICE OF HALF A LEMON

SMALL PIECE GINGER ROOT

GINGER ALE

Muddle the ginger in the bottom of a cocktail shaker. Pour all ingredients into a cocktail shaker filled with ice. Shake. Strain into a highball glass filled with ice.

HEALING SMOOTHIE

This drink protects and heals the stomach lining and is especially useful for making you feel better when you have a hangover.

1 KIWI FRUIT

1/4 CANTALOUPE

1 RIPE BANANA

Peel and cut up all of the fruit and place in a blender and blend until smooth. Serve in a tall glass, over ice if desired.

LIME LIFESAVER

Great for the morning after when you need to build strength. The ginger stimulates your system and the addition of vitamins from the carrots make this an essential day-after cocktail.

Makes 2 small glasses:

2 FRESH LIMES

6 MEDIUM CARROTS

FAIR-SIZED KNOB OF GINGER

2 APPLES

Cut the limes in half and juice them. Juice the carrots. Peel the ginger and juice it. Chop the apples and juice them. Combine all the juices, stir, and pour equally into two small tumblers.

LIVER RECOVERY

Apples are good for cleansing the liver and strawberries are good for the kidneys, so you have a double recovery whammy here.

6 FRESH STRAWBERRIES

2 GREEN APPLES

1 BANANA

Peel and core the apples and dice the strawberries. Peel the banana. Place all ingredients into a blender with a scoop of crushed ice. Blend until smooth. Serve in a highball glass.

MAESTRO'S MANGO MASHER

Mangoes are high in betacarotene and a good source of vitamins E, A, and C. This is a great health-reviving drink.

1/2 RIPE MANGO

JUICE OF 1 ORANGE

JUICE OF 1 LIME

LARGE HANDFUL FRESH RASPBERRIES

De-seed the mango and scoop out the flesh. Cut the citrus fruits in half and juice them. Put everything in the blender with a few ice cubes. Blend until the mixture is smooth. Serve in a large tumbler.

MIGHTY WONDER

I often wonder why I make this drink, but when the flavor hits me, I remember why—it's rich and delicious!

2 RED PEPPERS

5 TOMATOES

1 SMALL PIECE RED CHILI

DASH WORCESTERSHIRE SAUCE

2 TEASPOONS HONEY

BLACK PEPPER

Wash the peppers and cut in half, remove the seeds and the stalk, and cut the tomatoes into pieces. Juice the peppers and tomatoes with the chili. Stir the honey into the juice. Add the black pepper and Worcestershire sauce to taste. Serve over ice cubes in a highball glass.

NEAT BEET

Beetroot is a powerful cleanser and a great source of vitamin B6. It also combines well with carrots and most citrus fruits and is very good for your liver.

Makes 2 glasses:

2 LARGE CARROTS

1 SMALL BEETROOT

2 ORANGES (PREFERABLY BLOOD ORANGES)

Scrub the carrots and the beetroot. Cut off any stems, and slice into pieces. Cut the oranges in half and squeeze them. Pour the juice equally into two glasses. Juice the beet and carrots and add this mixture to the orange juice already in the glasses. Stir and drink quickly to prevent oxidation.

PAPA'S PAPAYA

This is one of my favorite fresh juices to wake up the body's system in the morning, especially if you've overindulged. It's full of vitamins and flavor.

Makes 2 large glasses:

1 PAPAYA

1 SMALL RIPE BANANA

6 MANDARIN ORANGES

Peel the papaya and scoop out the seeds. Discard. Chop the flesh roughly and place in the blender. Peel the banana, break into chunks, and add to the blender. Cut the mandarins in half and juice them. Add juice to the blender. Add a few ice cubes. Blend everything until smooth. Serve in large tumblers.

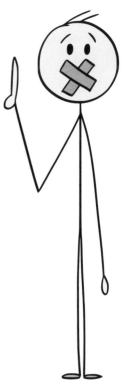

PEACH, RASPBERRY, AND REDCURRANT DELIGHT

Redcurrants can be tricky to find in the U.S., but usually show up in summer. These tiny red berries help make this drink sweet, full of flavor, and rich in vitamins A and C.

Makes 2 glasses:

1 RIPE PEACH

A HANDFUL RASPBERRIES

BERRIES FROM 20 REDCURRANT SPRIGS

Halve the peach, pull out the pit, and slice the peach flesh into a blender. Then add everything else. Add a splash of still water to help the blending process. Blend and serve in a highball glass.

PIÑA COPAYA

Papaya juice is rich in vitamins A and C, but its nutritional highlight is its enzymes, specifically papain, a protein digester. It's also a cleanser of the kidneys, liver, and intestines.

1 SMALL WEDGE PEELED PINEAPPLE (PEELED AND CORED)

1/2 PAPAYA, PEELED AND PITTED

ABOUT 6 OZ. (180 GRAMS) FRESH COCONUT, GRATED
(OR DRIED FLAKED COCONUT IF YOU CAN'T FIND FRESH)

ABOUT 4 OZ. (120ML) WATER

Blend all the ingredients until smooth. Serve in a tumbler with ice.

PINEMINT SMOOTHIE

This will wake up your digestive system gently first thing in the morning. I think it is one of the best hangover cures—easy on the stomach and great for when you have a headache.

Makes 2 highball glasses:

1/2 MEDIUM-SIZED PINEAPPLE

3/4 CUP OF NATURAL YOGURT

8 LARGE MINT LEAVES

DASH OF STILL MINERAL WATER

Peel the pineapple and dice the flesh. Place into a blender with the other ingredients. Add a dash of still water to help the blending process along. Blend until smooth. Serve, sip, and sigh.

PINK GRAPEFRUIT AND RASPBERRY WAKE-ME-UP

A light but powerful drink for breakfast, giving you energy (from the banana) and fizz from the fruits. Add ice if you like it long and smooth.

Makes 2 glasses:

2 LARGE HANDFULS RASPBERRIES

1 LARGE RIPE BANANA

JUICE OF 1 PINK GRAPEFRUIT

Rinse the raspberries and place them in a blender. Add the peeled banana and the grapefruit juice. Blend until smooth serve in a small glass.

PINO SMOOTHIE

A brilliant, red-colored drink that will make you drool with pleasure, and is good for you, too. It's a wonderful balance of sweet and sharp tastes.

1/4 LARGE FRESH PINEAPPLE

JUICE OF 1 ORANGE

2 HANDFULS RASPBERRIES

Peel the pineapple and dice the flesh. Blend with the orange juice and the berries. Add a few ice cubes and blend for a few seconds. Serve and enjoy.

PRAIRIE HEN

I'll admit, this is not pleasant to taste unless you like bitter drinks. It will, however, make you wary of having another hangover!

2 DASHES VINEGAR

2 TEASPOONS WORCESTERSHIRE SAUCE

1 FREE-RANGE EGG (DON'T BREAK THE YOLK!)

2 DASHES TABASCO SAUCE

SALT AND PEPPER, TO TASTE

Place the egg into a small wine glass. Add the remaining ingredients then drink it down in one gulp.

PRAIRIE OYSTER

An ancient hangover cure, it tastes vile but gives your body a shock and that can't be bad. This has eggs to bind it all together, tomatoes for vitamins, and olive oil to let it slip down easily.

VIRGIN OLIVE OIL

1 TABLESPOON KETCHUP

DASH WORCESTERSHIRE SAUCE

1 FREE-RANGE EGG YOLK

DASH WHITE WINE VINEGAR

DASH FRESHLY GROUND BLACK PEPPER

Lightly coat a small wine glass with olive oil and discard any excess. Add the ketchup and the egg yolk (don't break the yolk), season with the Worcestershire sauce, vinegar, and salt and pepper. Close your eyes and drink it down in one gulp.

RASPBERRY AND ORANGE SMOOTHIE

A deliciously smooth cocktail with a deep raspberry color.

5 HANDFULS RASPBERRIES

JUICE OF 1 ORANGE

3/4 CUP OF NATURAL YOGURT

6 MINT LEAVES

Rinse the raspberries and add them to a blender. Add the orange juice, yogurt, and mint leaves. Blend until smooth. Serve with ice in a highball glass.

. . . .

RED EYE

So-called because when you're making it, it appears like a red eye in a pool of juice!

1 FREE-RANGE EGG YOLK

SALT AND FRESHLY GROUND BLACK PEPPER

DASH OF LEMON JUICE

ABOUT 4 OZ. (120ML) CHILLED TOMATO JUICE

HALF A BOTTLE OF LAGER*

Pour the tomato juice and lemon juice into a beer glass and add the seasonings. Top up with lager and stir. Separate the egg and add the yolk only without breaking it. Drink up, and hope that your eyes clear! (*not quite nonalcoholic)

SANGRITA

A traditional Mexican drink that wakes up your taste buds.

4 OZ. (120ML) TOMATO JUICE

1-1/2 OZ. (45ML) FRESH ORANGE JUICE

1 TEASPOON CLEAR HONEY

1 OZ. (30ML) FRESH LIME JUICE

PINCH SALT

2 THIN SLICES CHILI PEPPER

1 TEASPOON FINELY CHOPPED WHITE ONION

FRESHLY GROUND BLACK PEPPER, TO TASTE

DASH WORCESTERSHIRE SAUCE

Pour all the ingredients into a shaker filled with ice and shake well. Then strain into a highball glass filled with ice. Garnish with a wedge of lime.

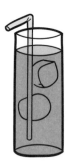

SENSATION

The perfect combination of sharp, sweet, and spicy flavors. Every ingredient will contribute to making you feel better.

3 OZ. (90ML) TOMATO JUICE

2 OZ. (60ML) PASSION FRUIT JUICE

2 OZ. (60ML) CARROT JUICE

JUICE OF HALF A LEMON

1 TEASPOON CLEAR HONEY

3-4 DASHES WORCESTERSHIRE SAUCE

Put all the ingredients into a cocktail shaker filled with ice. Shake. Strain into a tumbler.

THREE-BERRY DELIGHT

A drink of the deepest red color, this is a cleansing drink full of vitamin C.

1/2 CUP BLACKBERRIES

1/2 CUP RASPBERRIES

1/2 CUP REDCURRANTS

Rinse all the berries and place into a blender with ice. Blend until smooth. Serve in a wine glass.

TOMATO WONDER

Yes, despite its dubious beige color, this is definitely good for a hangover! The tomato gives it a clean, refreshing taste, and the radishes do what radishes do—which is wake up your palate.

4 FRESH TOMATOES

3 STALKS OF CELERY

4 RADISHES

1 HANDFUL PARSLEY

Place all the ingredients into a blender, along with some ice cubes, and blend until smooth. Drink the result!

VIRGIN LEA

My award-winning cocktail that's a perfect combination of sweet, spicy, and sharp flavors in one sip.

ABOUT 4 OZ. (120ML) TOMATO JUICE

2 OZ. (60ML) PASSION-FRUIT JUICE

1/4 YELLOW BELL PEPPER, DE-SEEDED AND SLICED

1 TEASPOON CLEAR HONEY

2 DASHES WORCESTERSHIRE SAUCE

Place the pepper slices in a blender and add the juices. Blend for ten seconds at low speed. Add the honey, Worcestershire sauce, and ice cubes. Blend at high speed for ten seconds. Pour through a strainer into a highball glass filled with ice cubes. Garnish with a cherry tomato and a basil leaf.

VIRGIN MARY

A truly spicy pick-me-up you can drink as a tonic whenever you feel the need.

5 OZ. (150ML) TOMATO JUICE

1 OZ. (30ML) FRESH LEMON JUICE

2 DASHES WORCESTERSHIRE SAUCE

SALT AND FRESHLY GROUND BLACK PEPPER

DASH TABASCO SAUCE

1 STICK CELERY

Pour the tomato juice into a highball glass filled with ice cubes. Season to taste with the spices. Stir well. Add the celery stick to use as a stirrer.

HOW TO DETOX A HANGOVER

The following program may sound daunting, but in terms of survival after a dire hangover, I strongly recommend that you try detoxing for a weekend at least: preferably one when you have no distractions and someone to pander to your every whim.

THE THREE-DAY DETOX PLAN

Too much rich food and drink, combined with a lack of exercise, leads to body overload, and your entire system becomes sluggish and congested. I recently devised this plan to cleanse the body and it's not that challenging. You will feel reinvigorated afterward. Try it and feel the difference.

One word of caution, however: Do not try this diet if you are under medical supervision, pregnant, or following another special diet.

In preparation for your detox, add a few drops of lavender essential oil to your wash cycle so that your bed linen is drenched in the aroma.

After this three-day period, carry on with light meals such as steamed chicken (without the skin), steamed fish (organic salmon is great, as is John Dory) and steamed vegetables. And by the way—it's best not to drink immediately after you've completed the program.

DAY ONE

Drink a cup of hot, boiled water first thing, followed throughout the day by only one kind of fruit, preferably apples or grapes. Drink your choice of mineral water when you feel hungry and don't want a piece of fruit.

This ought to be a restful day, so take it easy. Read the week's papers or flick through the latest issues of your favorite magazines, or go crazy on the Internet from your laptop.

In the evening, take a lavender bath, and when you have dried yourself, wrap up in a heavy bathrobe to assist toxin elimination through light sweating.

DAY TWO

You're not allowed any food at all today. Instead, drink hot, boiled water only, as much as you can take. This speeds up elimination and stimulates the lymph glands and the blood stream. Rest as much as you can—the housework can wait. You may experience tiredness, even headaches, and other small pains. In the evening, take a bath using rosemary oil for an antiseptic effect.

DAY THREE

Start with a cup of hot, boiled water. At about 11 a.m., drink a cup of vegetable juice, such as spinach mixed with carrot and diluted 50/50 with mineral water. If you don't like spinach, try beetroot—both are good for the liver.

Lunch can be a light salad of mixed green leaves and vegetables such as fresh spinach, zucchini, fresh green beans sliced thinly, and a variety of lettuce leaves. Squeeze a little lemon juice over this. One or two slices of organic whole grain bread will seem attractive at this point.

Afternoon tea can be an herbal variety or Earl Grey, with lemon.

For dinner, have some steamed brown rice with a fresh green vegetable, such as leeks, also steamed. Drink lots of mineral water throughout the day. In the evening, after dinner is digested, take a sea-salt bath to end the positive action.

NATURAL HERBAL CLEANSERS

ALFALFA SEEDS

Used in a Mexican tea remedy for a hangover headache. Steep one teaspoon of seed and a teaspoon of dried orange leaf in a cup of boiling water for five minutes. Strain into a cup and sip.

ANGELICA

Works as a tonic by improving liver function and stimulating digestion.

CAYENNE PEPPER

Soothing and restorative for the digestive system. Try sprinkling a small amount into a glass of still water and gargle. This will stimulate the production of saliva and other gastric juices to ease hangover-induced stomach troubles.

CHAMOMILE

Most commonly taken as a tea, this wonder herb is good for heartburn, stomachache, and general stress, among other complaints.

DANDELION

A godsend of a purifier. To treat a hangover, make a decoction using about 15 grams (half an ounce) of root to about 25 ounces (750ml) of water. Sip small quantities at frequent intervals throughout the day. To make a decoction the night before, place the root in a saucepan. Cover with cold water and bring to the boil. Simmer for about 20 minutes. Strain through a sieve into a jug. Cover and leave in a cool place.

EVENING PRIMROSE OIL

Thins the blood and dilates the vessels, thus easing that heavy thumping in your forehead.

FENNEL

Fennel tea is a soothing diuretic that will cleanse your system.

GINGER

Try chewing crystallized ginger to soothe the stomach and rebalance gastric juices. Similarly, ginger tea will help headache, heartburn, stomachaches, vomiting.

GINKGO BILOBA

Increases blood flow to the brain, so it's great for memory loss. Might be useful in remembering the name of the person you wake up with!

GINSENG

An all-purpose healer, it contains vitamins, minerals, amino acids, and balances blood-sugar levels. It is available as a tea or may be taken in pill form. Keep some in the hangover kit because it protects, strengthens, and tones the liver, boosts the immune system, and helps prevent toxic overload.

KUDZU ROOT

In Chinese, it means "drunkenness dispeller." Make a tea from equal parts of kudzu root, fresh ginger root, and umeboshi plum. All of the ingredients have an antispasmodic effect on the stomach muscles and help relieve nausea.

MILK THISTLE

Contains some of the most potent liver-cleansing properties around. The active nutrient is silymarin, which enhances the liver function and prevents free-radical damage. Available in tablet form. Take one with a meal each day.

PEPPERMINT

A familiar, pleasant-tasting remedy that relaxes the stomach muscles, calms down heartburn and stomachaches, and is a tried-and-tested remedy for nausea and vomiting. Take it as a tea.

ROSEMARY

Make an infusion of two heaped teaspoons of fresh rosemary in a cup of boiling water. Let it stand for five to ten minutes, then sip 2 oz. (50ml) every three hours.

SAFFRON

Use this spice in cooking to bring life back into your body. Buy the purest grade you can find, and add it to dishes per the recipe directions.

TURMERIC

A spice with antibacterial properties, turmeric has a beneficial effect on the liver, and stimulates the flow of bile. Take it as a capsule or in a curry.

INDEX OF ALCOHOLIC COCKTAILS

INDEX OF NON-ALCOHOLIC REMEDIES

ACKNOWLEDGMENTS

Thanks to all of my guests and friends who shared their favorite remedies with me and to my wife Sue for her continued support and patience.

To my Agent Fiona Lindsay of Limelight Management and Sterling Publishing for their continued interest in my work.

ABOUT THE AUTHOR

Fondly known as "The Maestro," Salvatore Calabrese is one of the world's leading bartenders, an award-winning global powerhouse—a consultant for select brands, a sought-after judge for worldwide competitions, and former President of the United Kingdom Bartenders' Guild. His bestselling books and barware products exemplify the quality, talent, and experience he brings to the industry.

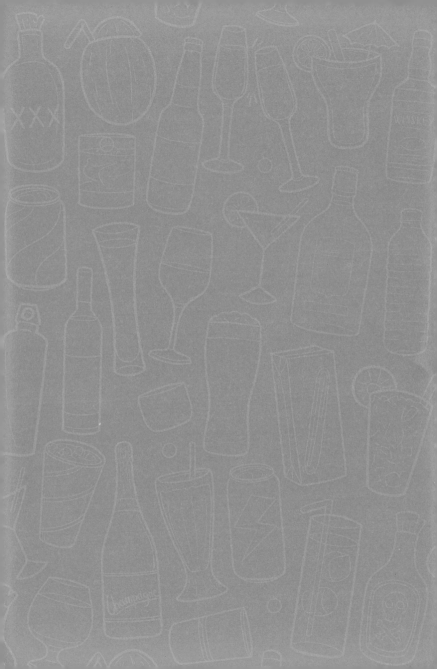